Tinky the Tyrannosaur
Copyright 2019 by Chris Rohaley, Chris 51
All story, layout and text by Chris 51
All art and color by Eddie Van Camp
All rights reserved. No part of this book may be reproduced or transmitted in any form or by any means, electronic or mechanical, including photocopying, recording, or by any information storage and retrieval system, without written permission of the publisher.
ISBN 978-1-5136-4619-0
ALPHA GEEK PUBLISHING
3585 Main St.
Springfield, OR 97478
CHRIS 51
email-Chris@chris51.com

for the scared...
May this story help give you the strength to
find your roar.

I will tell you of a story
told to me by a Woolly Mammoth,
so you know it is true.
You see Woollys cannot lie,
because if they do,
their trunk grows from one into two.

The Woolly named Willy
told me this tale from long ago.
Way back before the people came,
and before the dinosaurs had to go.

Everyone knows that
the Tyrannosaurus was the bravest around,
and the meanest dinosaur
in any dinosaur town.
And everyone knows that
a T-Rex has no friends
because they always end up
eating every one of them.

But this story is about a special little T-Rex boy,
a kid who wanted friends
and did not want to eat a single one of them.

His name was Tinker.
Tinker the tiny Tyrannosaur.
And Tinker was afraid,
afraid to talk to anyone he saw.

Everyday was just like the rest
Tinker would play in the jungle,
eating from the giant ju-ju berry nests.
And when he finally got tired,
in the mud pits he'd rest.

He would lay there and daydream
of having friends to play with
ohh how fun it would seem.
If only he could talk to them
without them thinking he was mean.

All the other kids stayed far away
except for just this one,
he just moved to the jungle,
just him and his mom.

His name was Tank.
Tank the Triceratops,
and Tank never saw a T-rex before.
So Tank tried to talk to the tiny Tyrannosaur.

Tinker saw him coming and was so scared.
The boy had horns on his head,
not just one, but three.
Tinker was so scared he ran and jumped,
right into a wallabee tree.

And that was a problem you see.
Because the roots of a wallabee tree
grow super fast, so one cannot flee.
And they already wrapped around Tinker,
they had circled around his little knees.

So when Tinker finally spoke,
he could only roar one word,
help.....
was all that Tank heard.

With the three giant horns on his head
Tank knew he could set the T-rex boy free.
He said, "I will help you,
but only if you will be friends with me."

Tinker was so happy to hear it
that his teeth grew
twice as big instantly.
He bit the roots
and chomped them off,
and Tinker set himself free.

This whole time I bet you did not know,
that when a boy T-rex is happy
his teeth begin to grow.

By now you might have guessed that Tinker has the biggest teeth of any Tyrannosaur around, because he has a best friend and is the happiest dinosaur in the whole dinosaur town.

THE END

www.ingramcontent.com/pod-product-compliance
Lightning Source LLC
Chambersburg PA
CBHW041121070526
44584CB00002B/231